A Fun Quiz

By Cameron Macintosh

Quin runs a quiz for kids.

Quin has a big quiz kit!

Quiz Kit

Let's do the quiz!

Can rats be pets?

Yes, rats **can** be pets!

You can pat them!

pet rat

On with the quiz!

Can pigs go to the Sun?

No, pigs can not go
to the Sun.

The Sun is too hot!

hot Sun

pig

Can dogs quack?

No, dogs can not quack!

Dogs yip and yap!

dog

This quiz is fun!

Is a quoll a fox with dots?

No! A quoll has dots,
but it is not a fox.

quoll

Are pugs big cats?

No, pugs are quick little dogs!

pugs

Do gulls have quills?

Yes, gulls have lots of quills!

A quill can be a pen, too!

gull

quill

That quiz was fun, Quin!

Quiz Kit

CHECKING FOR MEANING

1. Why can't pigs go to the Sun? *(Literal)*

2. What sounds do dogs make? *(Literal)*

3. Why do you think Quin's quiz was fun? *(Inferential)*

EXTENDING VOCABULARY

quiz	What is another word that has the same meaning as *quiz*? Have you ever been in a quiz? How many questions did you answer?
quack	Which animal makes this sound? Why do we say the word *quack* for the sound made by a duck?
quoll	What does a *quoll* look like? Which words could you use to describe a quoll? E.g. spotted, furry, long tail.

MOVING BEYOND THE TEXT

1. Have you seen children's quiz shows on TV? How are they played?

2. What information can you find about quolls? Where do they live? What do they eat? How do they move?

3. Make a list of all the types of pets owned by children in your class. Which is the most common?

4. Look at the sentence *A quill can be a pen, too!* Find out how people wrote with a quill in the past. Was it easy or hard to write using a quill?

SPEED SOUNDS

sh	ch	th	th	wh	qu	ph
		voiced	unvoiced			

PRACTICE WORDS

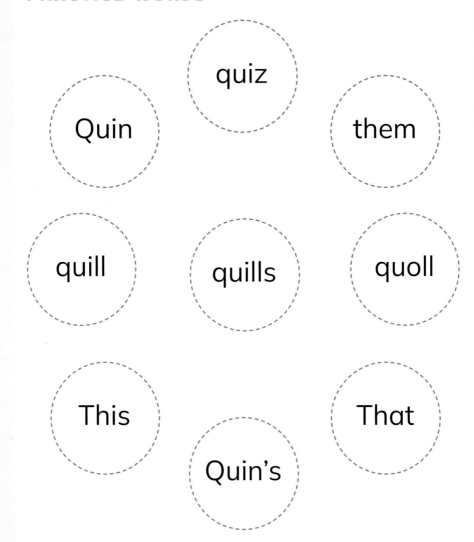

quiz

Quin

them

quill

quills

quoll

This

Quin's

That